I SAY! YOU SAY!
"This is what we ALL say!"

A Circle Time Tour

Through Concepts and the Curriculum

For Early Learners and their Teachers

By Ruth I. Dowell

Illustrations by Jim Cantwell

Another Pollyanna Production
Terre Haute, Indiana

The Author is available to conduct
workshops for schools and conferences.
For information, contact the publisher.

c1991 Ruth I. Dowell

Published by Pollyanna Productions, 4830 E. Poplar Drive
P. O. Box 3222, Terre Haute, IN 47803

All Rights Reserved. No part of this publication may be
reproduced without the prior written permission of the
publisher. Printed in the United States of America

INTRODUCTION

Children love pictures! And when they can predict or read the words that give pictures added meaning, the excitement grows! Through teacher-class interaction, this lavishly-illustrated book with its rhyming captions will provide such opportunities.

> DIRECTIONS FOR USE: Simply introduce these picture pages, *grouped and indexed for specific educational objectives,* with the stems provided and allow class members to verbalize *italicized endings.* With repeated use, however, expect children to eagerly provide more than the italicized portions, thereby maximizing the learning experience. (The predictability of the material will soon find children presenting the pages to each other!)

Whether their responses be spontaneous or read, children at all ability levels can participate in and benefit from these engaging, whole-language activities with equal satisfaction. Such lively "I Say...You Say" interaction will promote class productivity by instilling within its members a sense of confidence and self-direction that is the by-product of *"I can do it!"* Early learners will be drawn again and again to these provocative pages where, through the ease of interpretation, they can also begin to experience the joy, the exhileration of ...

"I can read it!"

About the Author (picture on back cover)

Background: B.S. and M.S. Degrees - Indiana State Teachers College (Terre Haute) Speech Pathology and Language Arts; Elementary Supervision Certified Classroom Teacher in Indiana and Florida. Resides in Terre Haute, IN, and Vero Beach, FL, when not on the road doing language-in-motion workshops nationwide.

In February, 1987, following the popularity of MOVE OVER, MOTHER GOOSE! (published by Gryphon House, Inc.) and, as a result of the many requests for workshop appearances, Ruth took early retirement from the public school system and now continues to write, publish and travel nationwide, providing in-service staff development programs, conference workshops, classroom visitations and other special-needs programs for schools and professional organizations.

TABLE OF CONTENTS

Introduction 3
About the Author 4

CONCEPTS and the CURRICULUM in RHYME

Everybody Look Around (Listening/Following Directions/Colors) 6
Once I Saw (Observation) 7
The Pig is Skinny (Opposites/Adjectives) 19
Hound Dog (Patterning/Cadence) 37
If I Heard (Fun With Words) 49
"Oink!" Said the Pig (Animal Sounds) 59
If a Lion Comes to Roar (Animal Trademarks/Action Words) 69
We Belong Together (Things That Go Together) 87
In a House Am I (Animal Habitats/Position Phrases) 109
If You Have Two Ears to Hear (Conditional Response) 120

Everybody Look Around

(Listening, Following Directions, Colors)
Tune: If You're Happy and You Know It

Everybody look around, clap your hands: *(one, two!)*
If your eyes see something blue, say, *("I do!")*
If your eyes see something black, gently pat somebody's back.
If your eyes see something brown, sit back down. *(Say, "I'm down!")*

If you've ever seen a pup, stand back up. *(Say, "I'm up!")*
If you've ever seen a cow, take a bow right now!
If you've ever seen a horse, you can say, "Of course." *("Of course!")*
If you've ever seen a cat, tip your hat like that!

If you've ever eaten corn, beep your horn. *("Beep, beep!")*
If you've ever eaten meat, stomp your feet!
If you've ever eaten hay, you're a horse! *("A horse, you say?!")*
If you've ever eaten cake, give a shake. *(Shake, shake!)*

If you've ever combed your hair, show me where. *("Right there!")*
If you've ever washed your face, run in place: win that race!
If you've ever caught a ball, stand up straight and stand up tall.
If you've ever played a game, say my name. *(Teacher's name)*

If your eyes see something pink, make them blink. *(Blink, blink)*
If your eyes see something red, nod your head.
If your eyes see something green, lick your lips until they're clean.
If your eyes see something white, say, "All right." *("ALL RIGHT!")*

Once I Saw

(Observation)

A Unicorn

A Beaver   A Cobra
A Hootowl   A Robin
A Kookaburra   A Lion
A Crow   A Mamma Bear
A Frog   A Dinosaur

Once I saw a unicorn flying through the air.
Blinked my eyes and looked again; then, he wasn't there!

Once I saw a beaver building him a dam.
"*Hurry, Mr. Beaver!*" Said the beaver, "*I AM!*"

Once I saw a hoot owl perched in a tree.
"Hoot-a-little, hoot owl; talk to me!"

Once I saw a kookaburra sitting on a fence.

Never saw him there before and haven't seen him since!

Once I saw a frog with a voice down deep.
"Noisy Mr. Bullfrog, go to sleep!"

Once I saw a crow eating corn on-the-cob.
"Wake up, Mr. Scarecrow! Do your job!"

Once I saw a cobra resting in a tree.

I saw him; but, I made sure he didn't see me!

Once I saw a robin hopping on the lawn.
Found a juicy worm and then he was gone.

Once I saw a lion chewing on a bone.
If you see a lion, better let him alone!

Once I saw a mama bear sleeping in a cave.
"Little bitty bear cub, better behave!"

Once I saw a dinosaur...you know that isn't true.
I couldn't see a dinosaur and neither could you!

The Pig is Skinny

(Opposites, Adjectives and Prepositions)

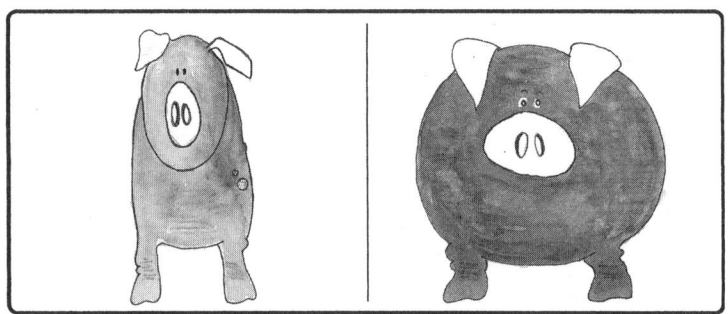

The Hog *is Fat!*

Rats are Large
Earth is Near
Kite is Low
Block is Square
Rabbit is Fast
Girl is Short
Day is Light
Smoke Goes Up

Stair has a Bottom
My Car is Old
Door Can Open
Lemon is Sour
Ice is Cold
Water is Wet
Pillow is Soft
Boy is a "He"

skinny **fat**

The pig *is skinny*. The hog *is fat*.

How did the hog ever get like that?

large   **small**

The rats *are large*.   The mice *are small*.

How would you, how could you catch them all?

near **far**

The earth *is near*. The moon *is far*.

Where do you, where do you think you are?

low   **high**

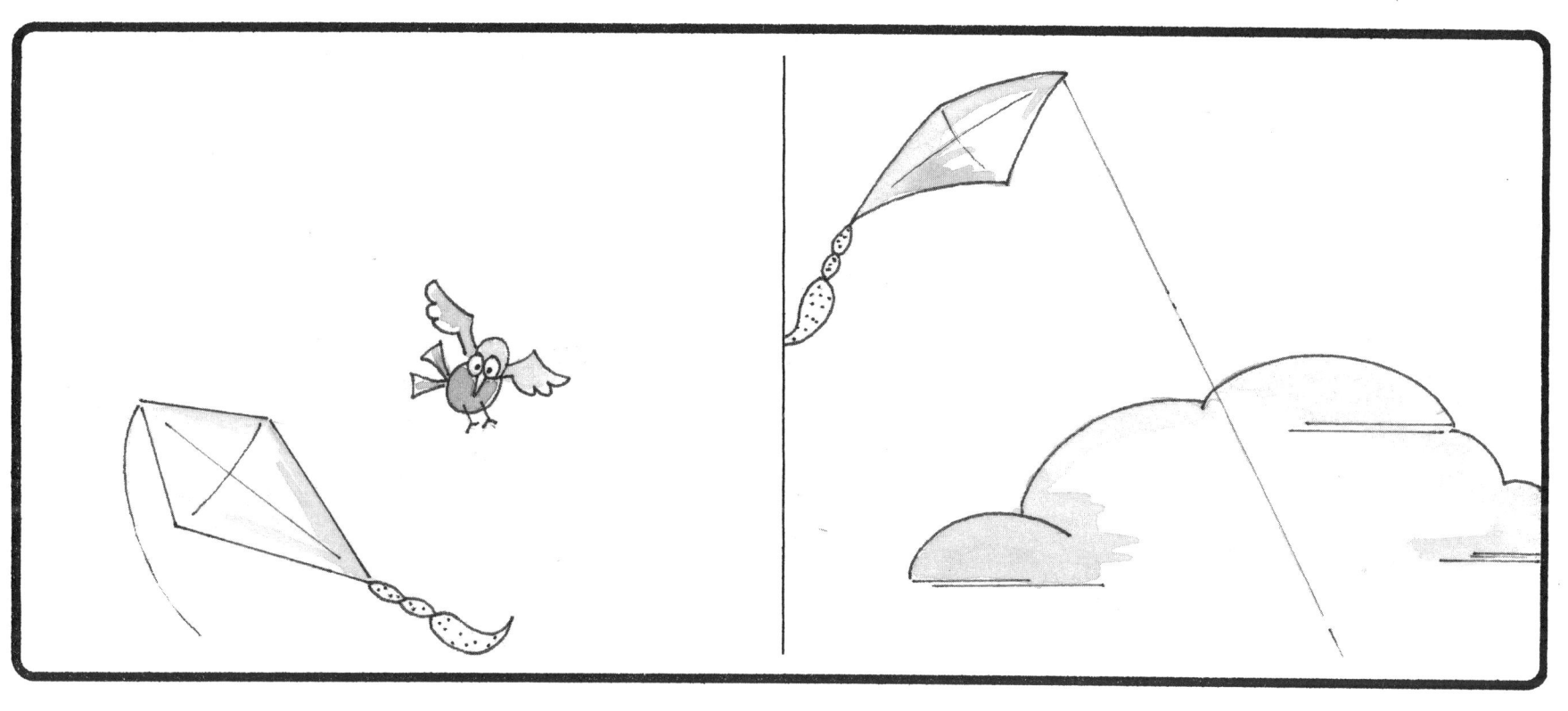

The kite *is low*.   The kite *is high*.

Will it go, will it go up in the sky?

square   **round**

The block *is square*.   The ball *is round*.

Which of the two could you bounce on the ground?

fast   **slow**

The rabbit *is fast*.   The turtle *is slow*.

Who'll win the race? Raise your hand, if you know!

short **tall**

The girl *is short*.   The boy *is tall*.

Measure them both with a mark on the wall.

light **dark**

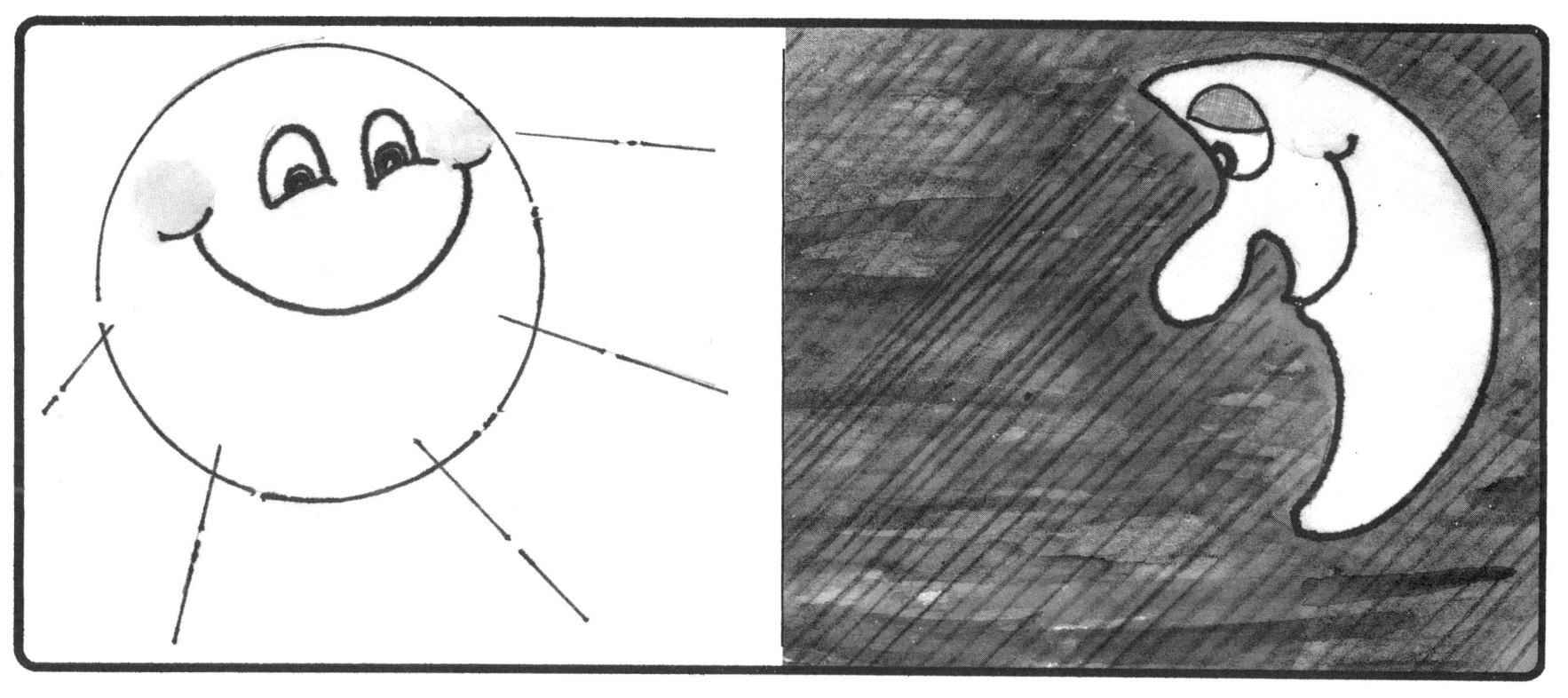

The day *is light*.   The night *is dark*.

If you do, when do you go to the park?

up **down**

The smoke *goes up*.   The rain *comes down*.

How is the weather on your side of town?

bottom **top**

A stair has *a bottom*.   ...and also *a top*.

If you get tired in the middle, you stop.

old   **new**

My car *is old*.   Your car *is new*.

It would be fun to go riding with you.

open **close**

A door *can open*   A door can *close*.

In comes your father, then out he goes.

sour   **sweet**

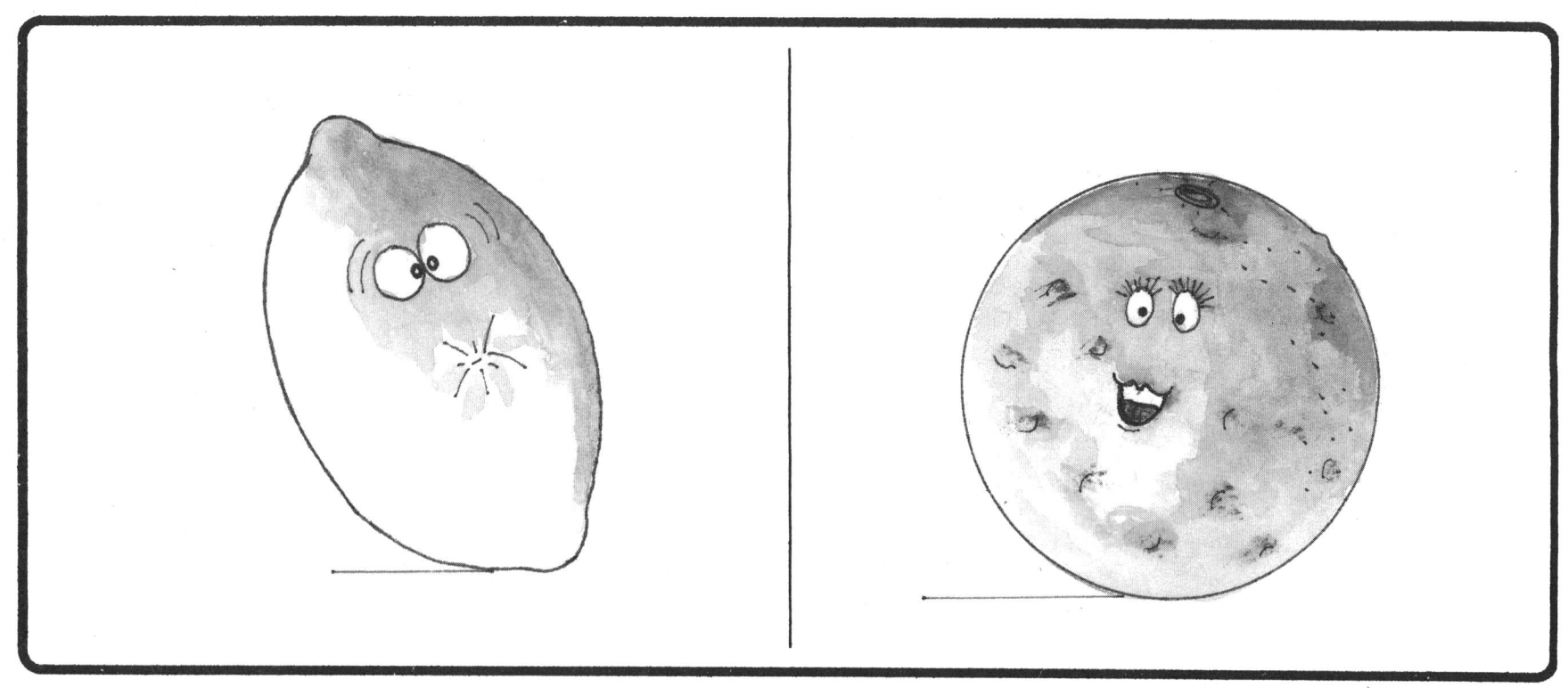

A lemon *is sour*.   An orange *is sweet*.

Which of the two would you like to eat?

cold   **hot**

The ice *is cold*.   The fire *is hot*.

Would you go, should you go touch them or not?

wet   **dry**

The water *is wet*.   The towel *is dry*.

Hope you don't get soap in your eye!

soft **hard**

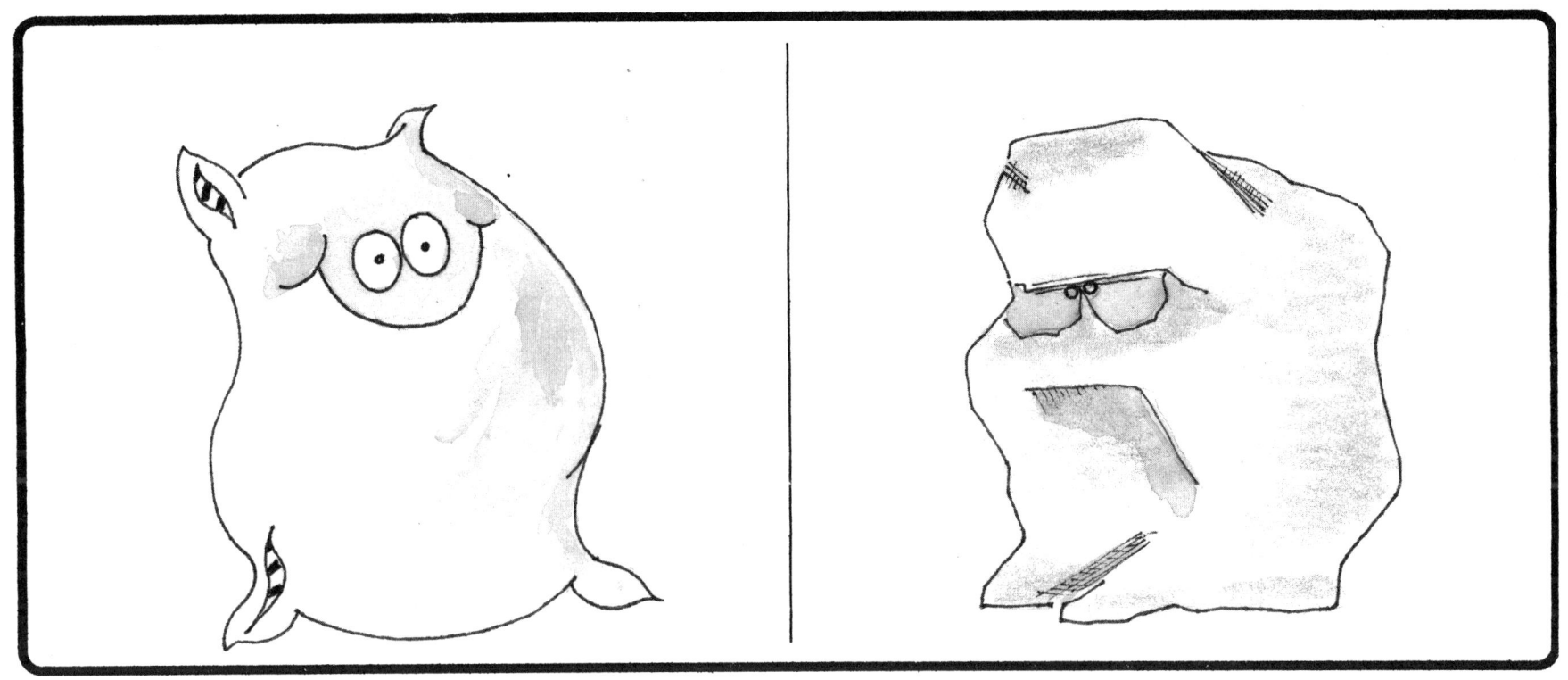

A pillow *is soft*.   A rock *is hard*.

Which of the two could you find in the yard?

he   **she**

A boy is *a "he."*   A girl is *a "she."*

What do you see when you look at me?

Hound Dog

(Patterning/Cadence)

Hound Dog had a flea.

Bull Frog
Brown Bear
Firefly
June Bug
Blackbird

Barn Owl
Fat Rat
Bull Moose
Sly Fox
Old Mule

Hound Dog

Hound dog had-a-flea: he-had a flea;
*He had-a-flea; now, the flea's **on me!***

Bull Frog

Bull Frog caught-a-fly: he-caught a fly;
*He caught-a-fly, as the fly **flew by!***

Brown Bear

Brown Bear made-a-wish: he-made a wish;
*He made-a-wish, and he caught **a fish**!*

Firefly

Firefly lit-a-light: he-lit a light.
*He lit-a-light with his tail **last night**!*

June Bug

June Bug flew-away: he-flew away.
*He flew-away on a sum-**mer day**!*

Blackbird

Blackbird ate-the-corn: he-ate the corn.
*He ate-the-corn in the ear-**ly morn**!*

Barn Owl

Barn Owl caught-a-mouse: he-caught a mouse.
*He caught-a-mouse in a haun-**ted house**!*

Fat Rat

Fat Rat gnawed-the-rope: he-gnawed the rope.
He gnawed-the-rope till the old **rope broke!**

Bull Moose

Bull Moose pulled-a-tooth: he-pulled a tooth.
*He pulled-a-tooth, pulled a loose **moose tooth**!*

Sly Fox

Sly Fox chased-a-hen: he-chased a hen.
*He chased-a-hen in the chick-**en pen**!*

Old Mule

Old Mule wouldn't-go: he-wouldn't go.
*He wouldn't-go, till I told **him**, '**Whoa!**'*

If I Heard

(Fun with Words: Reason/Humor)

A Turtle Yodel

A Lion Cryin'
A Badger Begging
A Robin Sobbin'
An Eagle Giggle

A Tiger Tattle
A Rabbit "rribit"
A Panther
A Parrot Swear It

If I heard a turtle yodel, he'd go, *"Yodel-odle-ee!"*
Would you ever hear a turtle yodel? No-sir-ee!

If I heard a lion cryin', would he cry all over me?

Would you ever hear a lion cryin'? No sir-ee!

If I heard a badger begging, would he beg a bite from me?
Would you ever hear a badger begging? No-sir-ee!

If I heard a robin sobbin', I would set him on my knee.
Would you ever hear a robin sobbin'? No-sir-ee!

If I heard an eagle giggle, I would giggle more than he!
Would you ever hear an eagle giggle? No-sir-ee!

If I heard a tiger tattle, would the tiger tell on me?
Would you ever hear a tiger tattle? No-sir-ee!

If I heard a rabbit "rribit," on a lily pad he'd be!
Would you ever hear a rabbit "rribit?" No-sir-ee!

If I telephoned a panther, would the panther answer me?
Would you ever telephone a panther? No-sir-ee!

If I heard a parrot swear it, I would know it had to be!
Would you ever hear a parrot swear it? No-sir-ee!

"Oink!" Said the Pig

(Animal Sounds)

"Oink!" said the pig to the old blue jay."

"Psst!" Said the Snake   "Moo...," Said the Cow
"Peep!" Said the Chick   "Quack!" Said the Duck
"Arf!" Said the Dog   "Honk!" Said the Goose
"Oink!" Said the Pig   "Meow!" Said the Cat

Snakes hiss.

"*Psst!*" said the snake to the rat in the loft.
"*Don't you wish you could hiss that soft?*"

Chicks chirp.

"Peep, peep, peep!" said the chick to the coot.
"Don't you wish you could chirp that cute?"

Dogs bark.

"*Arf!*" said the dog to the old tom cat.
"*Don't you wish you could bark like that?*"

Pigs grunt.

"Oink!" said the pig to the old blue jay.
"Don't you wish you could grunt that way?"

Cows moo.

Moooo!

"*Moo...,*" said the cow where the donkey stood.
"*Don't you wish you could moo that good?*"

Ducks quack.

"Quack!" said the duck to the sheep in the fold.
"Don't you wish you could quack that bold?"

Geese honk.

"*Honk!*" said the goose to the barnyard crowd.
"*Don't you wish you could honk that loud?*"

Cats mew.

"*Meow!*"   said the cat to the three blind mice.
"*Don't you wish you could mew that nice?*"

So, they hiss, chirp, bark and they grunt and they moo
And they quack and they honk and they mew.

Can you?

("People talk!")

If a Lion Comes to Roar

(Animal Trademarks & Action Phrases)

If a Lion Comes *to Roar*

Turtles Snap
Rabbits Race
Chickens Peck
Owls Look
Grizzlys Hug
Monkeys Climb
Tigers Eat
Bunnies Hop

Kangaroos Box
Parrots Talk
Panthers Pounce
Ponies Prance
Piggys Root
Badgers Dig
Roosters Crow
Eagles Fly

If a lion comes *to roar*, say...

"That's what a JUNGLE'S for!"

If a turtle comes *to snap*, say...

"I think you need a nap!"

If a rabbit comes *to race*, tell him...

"This is not the place!"

If a chicken comes *to peck,* say...

"Wear something 'round your neck."

If an owl comes *to look*, say...

"*Take time to read a book.*"

If a grizzly comes *to hug*, tell her...

"First, go sweep the rug."

If a monkey comes *to climb*, tell him...

"This is not the time."

If a bunny comes *to hop*, say...

"I'll tell you when to stop."

If a tiger comes *to eat*, say...

"You have to wash your feet!"

If a kangaroo comes *to box*, tell him...

"Hey, pull up your sox!"

If a parrot comes *to talk*, say...

"I'd rather take a walk."

If a panther comes *to pounce*, tell him...

"Here's a ball to bounce."

If a pony comes *to prance*, tell him...

"You forgot your pants!"

If a piggy comes *to root*, tell him...

"Here's a horn to toot!"

If a badger comes *to dig*, say...

"Don't make the hole too big."

If a rooster comes *to crow*, say...

"I think you'd better go!"

If an eagle comes *to fly,* say...

"Be sure to wave goodbye!"

We Belong Together

(Things That Go Together)

"I'm the hands. You're the clock."

Grapes and Vine	Handle and Pot
String and Kite	Sail and Boat
Nest and Bird	Saucer and Cup
Glass and Ice	Glove and Hand
Gate and Fence	Nut and Shell
Hive and Bee	Soup and Spoon
Foot and Shoe	Jam and Bread
Bat and Ball	Leaf and Tree
Lock and Key	Head and Hat
Fork and Knife	Cushion and Chair

"*I'm the hands. You're the clock.*"
Said the clock, "*Tick, tock!*"

"We're the grapes. You're the vine."
Said the vine, "Where's Number 9?"

"I'm a nest. You're a bird."
Said the bird, *"So I heard."*

"I'm the string. You're the kite."
Said the kite, *"Hold tight!"*

"I'm the glass. You're the ice."
Said the ice, "That's nice!"

"*I'm a gate. You're a fence.*"
Said the fence, "*Makes sense.*"

"I'm a hive. You're a bee."
Said the bee, *"Lucky me!"*

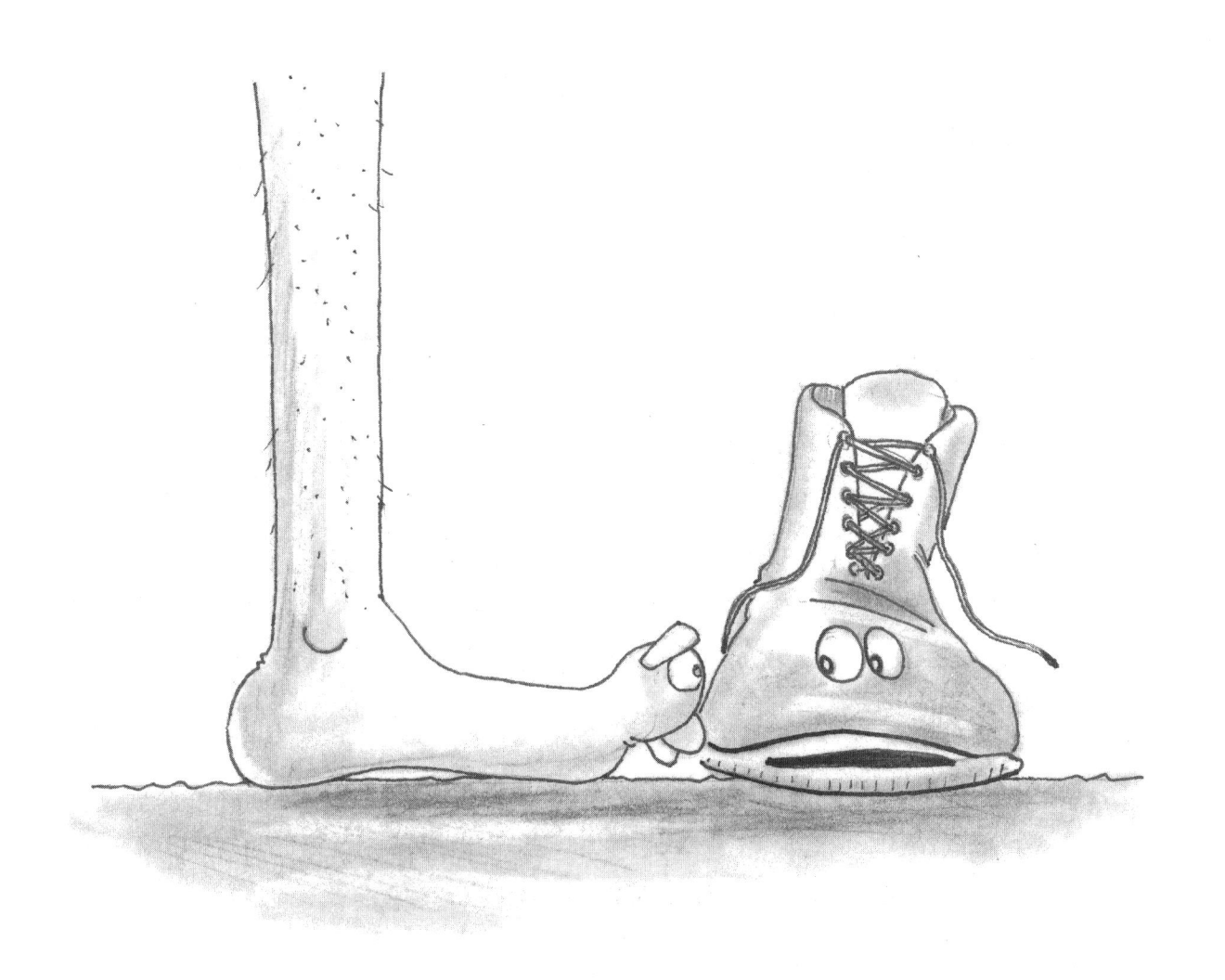

"I'm a foot. You're a shoe."
Said the shoe, "*Good for you!*"

"I'm a bat. You're a ball."
Said the ball, "You're tall!"

"I'm a lock. You're a key."
Said the key, *"Who, me?"*

"I'm a fork. You're a knife."
Said the knife, "Whatta life!"

"I'm a handle. You're a pot."
Said the pot, *"I'm getting hot!"*

"*I'm a sail. You're a boat.*"
Said the boat, "*See me float!*"

"*I'm a saucer. You're a cup.*"
Said the cup, "*Fill me up!*"

"I'm a glove. You're a hand."
Said the hand, "I understand."

"*I'm a nut. You're a shell.*"
Said the shell, "*I can tell!*"

"*I'm the soup. You're the spoon.*"
Said the spoon, "*Lunch at noon!*"

"I'm the jam. You're the bread."
Said the bread, "Who said?"

"I'm a leaf. You're a tree."
Said the tree, *"So I see."*

"I'm a head. You're a hat."
Said the hat, *"I know that!"*

"I'm a cushion. You're a chair."
Said the chair, *"Put 'er there!"*

In a House Am I

(Animal Habitats & Position Phrases)

In the grass *there's a snake*
In a hole *there's a mouse.*
In the yard *there's a dog*
  in the old doghouse.

On a leaf *there's a bug.*
In the air *there's a germ.*
In the woods *there's a snail.*
On the ground *there's a worm.*

In a nest *there's a bird.*
In a hive *there's a bee.*
In a web *there's a spider*
  looking down at me!

In a hutch *there's a rabbit.*
In a sty *there's a hog.*
In a coop *there's a chicken.*
In a pond *there's a frog.*

In the lake *there's a fish.*
In the sea *there's a whale.*
In the jungle *there's a monkey*
  with a funky tail!

In a den *there's a wolf.*
On the wall *there's a fly.*
In a cave *there's a bear.*
In a house *AM I!*

In the grass *there's a snake!* In a hole *there's a mouse!*

In the yard *there's a dog in the old doghouse!*

On a leaf *there's a bug*. In the air *there's a germ*.
In the woods *there's a snail* On the ground *there's a worm*.

In a nest *there's a bird*. In a hive *there's a bee*.

In a web *there's a spider looking down at me!*

In a hutch *there's a rabbit*. In a sty *there's a hog*.
In a coop *there's a chicken*. In a pond *there's a frog*.

In the lake *there's a fish*. In the sea *there's a whale*.

In the jungle *there's a monkey with a funky tail!*

In a den *there's a wolf*. On a wall *there's a fly*.
In a cave *there's a bear*...

In a house am I!

If You Have Two Ears

(Conditional Response)

Tune: If You're Happy and You Know It

If you have two ears to hear, clap your hands! *One! Two!*
If you think a cow can chew, say, "I do!" *("I do!")*
If a dog could have a flea, start with 1 and count to 3. *("1-2-3!")*
If a turtle has a fin, clap again!
If a cat could say, "Meow," take a bow right now!
If a camel has a hump, time to jump. (Jump, jump!)
If a polar bear is black, put your hands behind your back!
If a tiger has a claw, say, "Hurrah!" ("Hurrah!")

If a stinger has a bee, point to me!
If a monkey ever swings, spread your wings. Like this!
If a mule would ever kick, give your upper lip a lick!
If a rooster lays an egg, shake your leg!
If a squirrel climbs a tree, slap your knee. *"One, two!"*
If a crow would ever crow, touch your toe. Touch your toe!
If a crocodile is red, rub your stomach!...Pat your head!
If you think giraffes are tall, say, "That's all!"

"That's all!"